ACKNOWLEDGMENTS

The author and publisher wish to thank the people who read the manuscript of this book and made suggestions: Lewis Love, Great Neck, New York, Public Schools; Jane Sokolow, The New York Botanical Garden; Millicent Selsam, botanist and author; The Peanut Advisory Council; The Popcorn Institute; and the many young "helpers" who tried the experiments.

Other Books by Rose Wyler

The Giant Golden Book of Astronomy
Prove it!
Secrets in Stones [all written with Gerald Ames]
Real Science Riddles

FOREWORD

Science is a way of looking at the world around you and trying to understand how things work. Did you ever ask, "Why is the sky blue?" or "Why does a seed begin to grow?" or "What is a cloud?" Nearly everyone asks such questions, but you can do more than that. You can do real science experiments to help you find the answers.

This book will show you how to do experiments yourself. They are easy to set up at home or at school and they are fun to do. Although you will use peanut and popcorn seeds as you work, you will find out how all plants grow. Not only that—you will be developing the skills and ways of thinking of a scientist.

Lewis Love
Great Neck Public Schools
Long Island, New York

CONTENTS

6

What's Inside a Seed?

Long ago, when Indians roasted popcorn, they sometimes told children this story. Each kernel is a house with a little man inside. If you heat his house, he gets mad. He gets so mad, he tears it down. And that makes the popcorn pop.

Of course, no little men live in popcorn. Yet there is something alive in every kernel. It stays there—sometimes for years and years. But you can make it come out anytime you wish.

There is something alive in a peanut, too. It is like the living thing in popcorn—it is a baby plant, all ready to grow.

The true story of peanuts and popcorn has no ending, for both are seeds. Like all seeds, they make new plants that make new seeds that make new plants. And this goes on and on.

But let's start with one peanut seed and the baby plant hidden inside. To see it, take a raw peanut, not a roasted one. Slip the skin off, then split the peanut in half. At one end, there's a little bump. That's the baby plant, called an embryo (em-bri-o).

Look at the bump with a magnifying glass. Can you see the tiny leaves sticking out? The rest of the seed is stored food that the baby plant uses as it starts to grow.

You can buy raw peanuts in a supermarket or a health food store. Seed companies sell them, too. Keep the peanuts in a tightly closed jar and they will not spoil.

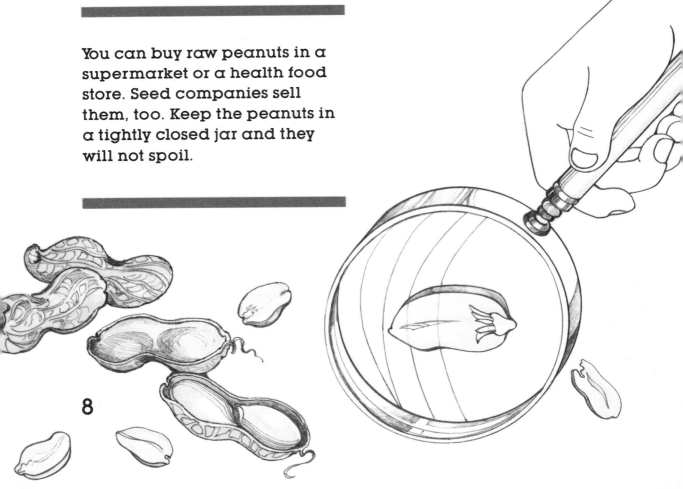

8

Dried but Alive

A popcorn kernel is full of stored food, too. Part of this food is yellow; part is white. The baby plant is inside the white part. The popcorn kernels that you buy are dry and hard, but the tiny plants in them are still alive.

If you soak some kernels overnight, you can take one and peel off the skin. Then you can see the tiny popcorn plant. This is how it looks through a magnifying glass.

When you eat peanuts or popcorn, you eat the food that has been stored for baby plants. In the peanut, this food is mainly fat. In popcorn, it is mainly starch. You use these foods too, as you grow.

New Plants from Old

A tiny popcorn plant will grow up into a big tall plant. Ears of corn will grow on it. After the ears are picked and dried, the corn kernels are taken off. These are the seeds that will make new popcorn plants.

The peanut plant is called a vine. It is a low plant and its new seeds form underground. When these peanuts are ripe, they can be dug up. New peanut plants will grow from them—unless someone eats them first!

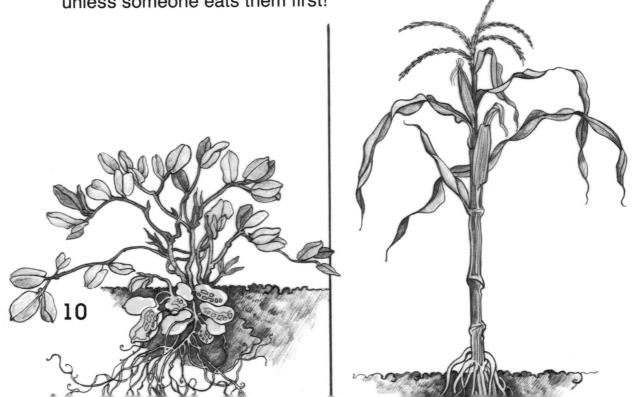

10

Seeds come in many different sizes and shapes. Apple and orange seeds and peach and avocado pits are all different kinds of seeds. So are peas and beans. The coconut is a seed too—the largest one of all. Different though they are, each of these seeds has a baby plant inside.

How can you make a baby plant come out of a seed? While the seed is dry, the plant stays inside. But give the seed water and see what happens.

Put a teaspoon of shelled raw peanuts in a jar. Add ten teaspoons of water, cover the jar, and let it stand overnight. The next day, see how big the peanuts are. Water has soaked into them, making them swell. Pour the water left in the jar into a cup and measure it. How many teaspoons are there? If nine are left, the spoonful of peanuts has soaked up one spoonful of water.

Water softens the food stored in the seed. The food is broken into tiny bits and is dissolved. A baby peanut plant can use this dissolved food, and if it gets the other things it needs, it will grow.

Popcorn Push-ups

Did you know popcorn can be a weight-lifter? The dry kernels can soak up a lot of water and as they swell, they press in all directions. If anything is on top of them, they push against it and lift it, as this experiment shows.

Fill a small plastic tumbler or jar with raw kernels. Then add water right up to the rim. Cover the top with a plastic dish. After an hour, check the experiment. You will see that the swollen kernels are lifting the dish. Next morning, check the experiment again. Where is the dish? The kernels have pushed it off!

Try the experiment with other kinds of dried seeds, such as beans or peas. Do you get the same results?

Outdoors, seeds are weight-lifters, too. When a seed swells with water, pressure builds up in it. The seed pushes aside soil, making room for the baby plant's root and stem. Soon the root takes in water, and as the water rises, pressure builds up in the stem. The pressure becomes so strong that the seedling can push its way out of the ground, and up it comes.

Seeds' Needs

What else besides water do seeds need to make them grow? Here's a way to find out.

Line a jar with paper towels. Slip five raw peanuts between the glass and paper on one side of the jar, and five popcorn grains on the other side. Add two tablespoons of water, then cover the jar.
Set up a second jar just like the first one. Keep one in the refrigerator and one in a warm place for five days.

Look at the seeds every day. Do the seeds in both jars sprout?

14

You find that seeds sprout when they are warm, but not when they are cold. This is true of all seeds.

Outdoors, during the cold winter, seeds do not sprout. They start to grow only when warm weather comes.

Starter Gardens

Indoors, raw peanuts and popcorn will sprout at any time of the year.

It's easy to make little gardens for these plants, for they will start growing without soil.

For the gardens, use two pans. Line each pan with several paper towels. Spread *raw* peanuts around one pan and put popcorn in the other. Water the seeds—get the towels very wet. Then cover each pan with clear plastic.

Keep the pans in a warm place and watch your gardens grow.

16

Seedlings Start to Grow

Seeds change very fast in a starter garden. First the seeds swell and the skin breaks. In a few days, roots push out from one end. Soon after that, stems sprout from the other end. Now the baby plants are seedlings.

The seedlings grow and grow. They get along without soil because they are living on the food stored in the seeds. As water soaks into the seed, the food is dissolved. It is broken into tiny bits that become part of the sap. The sap flows into the new roots and stems, bringing them everything they need.

Green Peanuts!

After three days, the peanuts look very strange. They have turned green. Is anything wrong? No, sprouting peanuts always turn green. The two halves open out, and now that they are green, they are called seed leaves. The baby plant that lies between them is alive and well.

Can the plant grow without seed leaves?

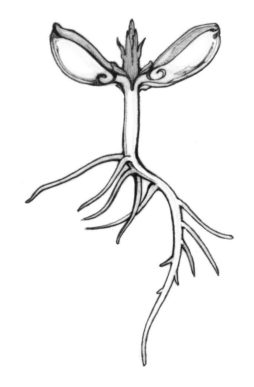

To find out, take three little peanut seedlings, and three paper cups filled with soil. Snip both seed leaves off the first seedling. Snip just one off the second, and leave both seed leaves on the third seedling.

Place each plant in a cup with the root pointing down, water the soil and label each cup. Then keep the plants in a warm place for a week.

Does the plant without seed leaves die? Does the plant with two seed leaves grow bigger than the plant with only one?

19

At first, baby plants need the food stored in seed leaves. They live on it until they get real leaves. The real leaves will make food, and then the seedlings will use this new food.

Fuzzy Popcorn!

In the popcorn garden, white fuzz covers the roots. But don't worry. Nothing is wrong. Look at a root with a magnifying glass, and you see that the fuzz is really hundreds of hairs. Each one is a branch of the root. It takes in water, just as the main part of the root does. Growing popcorn needs lots of water, and gets it through the tiny root hairs.

Peanuts and popcorn show how most seeds sprout. There are two main types of seeds. One type is like the peanut. It has two seed leaves and splits when it sprouts. The other type is like popcorn. It has only one seed leaf and it doesn't split.

20

Growth Checkup

Of course, you want your seedlings to hurry up and become grown-up plants. And they will, in time. While the stems are still small, the roots are growing very fast.

How much did you grow last year? An inch? If you grew two inches, you grew a lot. But the roots of your seedlings can grow that much in *one week.*

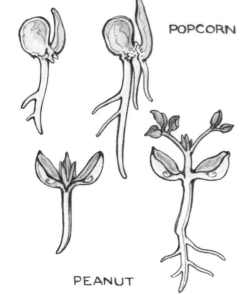

POPCORN

PEANUT

Pick a popcorn grain that has just sprouted, and separate it from the others. After three days, measure its root, and three days later, measure it again. Do the same thing with a sprouting peanut.

Is this what you find? In the first three days, the roots grow an inch, and in the next three days, another inch.

You wouldn't want to grow *that* fast. If you did, you would be a giant in less than a year!

Just how does a root grow? From the top? From the bottom? Or does all of it grow? The answer may surprise you.

Take the root of the popcorn seedling from the last experiment—or a seedling like it. Using a ball point pen, mark the root with dots.

Put the seedling in a jar lined with wet paper towels. Place it with its root hanging down next to the glass. Now see what happens to the spaces between the dots.

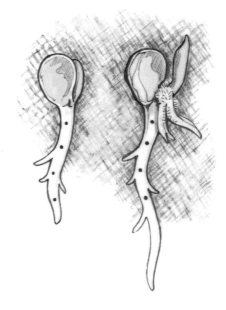

After a few days you can tell that only one part of the root is growing. What part is that? The tip.

All roots grow that way.

A chemical, called a hormone, forms in the root tip and makes it grow longer. You can get this chemical in stores that sell plants. Sometimes it is called a root promoter; it speeds up root growth in all plants. Hormones that promote growth form in your body, too. One kind makes your bones grow longer.

Down They Go

When seedlings grow in soil, their roots go downward. If something is in the way, they move around it, and keep on going down. Even if you point roots up, they turn back down.

Try this. Take the top off a plastic food carton and put several very wet paper towels on it. Lay four popcorn seedlings on this bed, each with its roots pointing in the same direction. Cover them with plastic wrap and seal it so that water doesn't leak out.

Now stand the bed on edge.

Turn it every two days and you will see that the roots of the seedlings turn too. They always turn downward.

After a week, the roots make an interesting pattern.

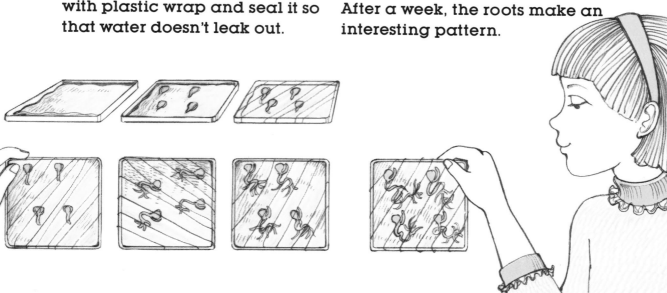

Other parts of plants grow upward and sideways. Only roots go downward. Why is that? Scientists say the growth chemical in the tips reacts to the earth's gravity. This force pulls downward; so roots grow downward.

Can you fool roots and make them grow up, instead of down? To find out, scientists cut the root tips off some seedlings, then placed them in special beds with their roots pointing upward. The beds were put in a dark, warm room and the seedlings grew. For a while the roots kept on pointing upward—but only for a while. When the new tips formed on them, the tips reacted to gravity. And then all the roots grew downward.

How would roots grow in a space ship, in zero gravity, where there is no up or down? That's an experiment some astronauts have tried. But more experiments are needed before we know how plants grow in space.

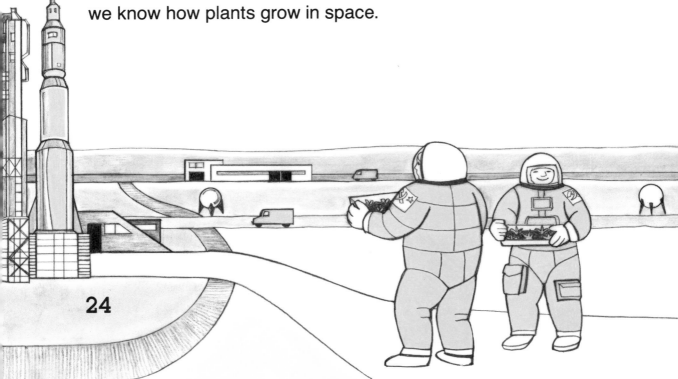

Lively Stems and Leaves

How is your popcorn garden doing? By now the leaves may be a few inches high. Do they touch the plastic wrap? If they bend, take off the wrap and they will quickly straighten up.

Stems and leaves move in other ways, too. If you place the garden near a window, the stems and leaves will grow toward the light. Turn the garden around and again they bend toward the light.

1

2

3

4

Try this, too. Plant a popcorn seedling in a paper cup. Then take an empty milk carton and cut a hole near the top. Open the top and put the cup with the seedling at the bottom. Close the carton so that the inside is dark. Stand the carton in a warm place and in a day or two leaves poke out of the hole.

It seems as if the plant is playing peekaboo!

If you try the "peekaboo" experiment with other plants, you find their leaves will also turn toward the light.

Leaves die without light. They lose their green color and cannot make food for the plant. What kind of food do they make? Sugar is one kind. When they have light and warmth, leaves make food from a gas in the air called carbon dioxide and from water. They stop working in the dark.

By day, the green in the leaves traps rays from the sun. The sun rays provide energy. The energy is then used to change water and carbon dioxide gas into sugar. This is called photosynthesis (fo-to-sin-thi-sis). Only green plants make food by photosynthesis. If you add carbon dioxide to water, the gas makes bubbles and all you get is soda water!

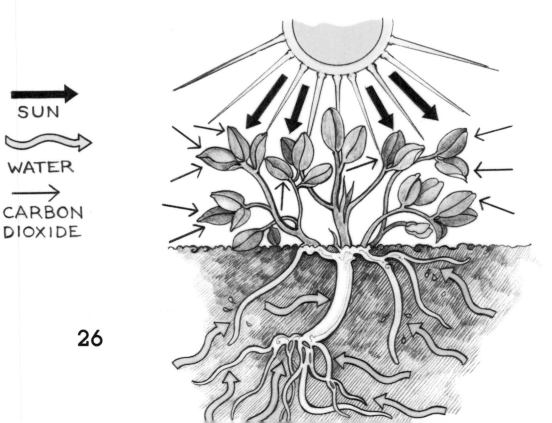

SUN

WATER

CARBON DIOXIDE

Transplant Time

When seedlings have lots of leaves, it's time to take them out of the starter garden. They need minerals as well as water now, and they can get both from soil. To keep the seedlings alive, you must transplant them.

First dig up some good soil, or buy some. Instead of a flower pot, use a milk carton or plastic container for each seedling. Cut holes near the bottom and put the container on a dish. Fill the container with soil and water it. Set your seedling in the wet soil. And there! It's transplanted.

Now the seedling is ready for a new life. It is a young plant that can make food all by itself.

Night Work for Leaves

The more light the leaves get, the more food they make and the faster the plant grows. That's why some people keep their plants under electric light at night.

You can get popcorn leaves to work at night too, if you have a lamp with a fluorescent bulb. Fluorescent light does not burn the leaves. It just tricks them into working as they do in the daytime.

Do you have some popcorn seedlings? Then try this. Take eight seedlings—all about the same size. Put four in one pot and four in another just like it. Keep one pot under fluorescent light every night, but set it next to the other pot during the day. Keep the soil in both pots moist. After a week, which plants are bigger?

If you don't have seedlings, start with raw kernels, and keep one pot under light every night. You may get super seedlings.

Young peanut and popcorn plants are very pretty. Their leaves will make food and they will grow indoors if you keep them in a sunny place and water them once or twice a week. Before long they may need to be transplanted again.

A popcorn plant should have a big pot or pail of its own, for it may grow quite tall. Peanuts do not grow as tall, so you can plant several together in a big container.

To transplant your plants, first prepare the container. Use a large pail or a cardboard carton lined with a thick plastic bag. Cover the bottom with pebbles and put in soil. Cut away the old containers from the plants, then move them with soil around their roots. Set them about four inches apart, so each will have plenty of room.

EARTH
PEBBLES
PLASTIC LINER

Both the peanut and popcorn plants will grow better if you add minerals to the soil every two weeks. You can get the minerals in a liquid called plant food. Add the food according to directions on the bottle. Keep the soil moist and you will have a fine mini-farm.

30

The Peanut Patch

Outdoors, it's easy to start a peanut patch. Do it late in April or May, and use raw, shelled peanuts as seed. Plant them two inches deep in rows four inches apart. In about a week, little green shoots are poking out of the ground. Four weeks later, flower buds open, but the flowers last only a day. Then their stems swell and form long pegs that work their way into the ground. The pegs get bigger and in about two months, they are ripe peanuts, ready to be dug up.

Can you get peanuts from plants grown indoors? You may, if they bloom. But indoors or outdoors, the time between planting and harvesting is more than four months.

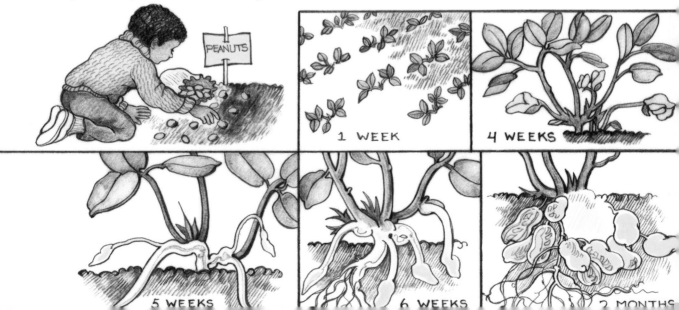

1 WEEK

4 WEEKS

5 WEEKS

6 WEEKS

2 MONTHS

Travels of the Peanut

You can get peanuts almost everywhere today, but long ago, no one in this country grew them. No one had even heard of them.

Peanuts came here in a roundabout way. For centuries, Indians had been growing peanuts in South America. Explorers from Spain learned of them there. The Spaniards liked them so much they took some home to plant. Later, they took peanuts along on voyages to Africa, and Africans began to eat peanuts, too.

When Africans were brought to America as slaves, peanuts were their main food on the voyage. Some slaves saved a few and hid them in their hair, then planted them here to avoid starving. And that's how peanuts traveled all the way from South America to Spain to Africa to this country.

Dr. Carver's Work

For a long time, no one thought of making anything from peanuts. People just ate them, or they let their pigs dig them up and eat them. Then farmers sold the pigs, instead of the peanuts.

Could peanuts be used in other ways? One man thought so—the scientist George Washington Carver. He was the son of a slave. In his laboratory, Dr. Carver experimented with every part of the peanut—the shell, skin, and seed. From them he made oils, dyes, animal food, paste, flour, wall board, and almost 300 other products. Mills began making many of these products and farmers began selling tons of peanuts to the mills. Now peanuts are the biggest crop in the south.

Peanuts are grown in every southern state from Virginia to California. The size of the entire crop is almost as big as the wheat crop. It is over one and a half million tons!

Peanut Products

Today, when peanuts go to a mill, big rollers squeeze oil out of them. Most of this oil goes into bottles to be sold as vegetable oil. Nearly all the rest of the peanut seed is made into feed for cows and pigs.

Every part of the peanut is used—even the shells. Some of the shells are ground into mulch that farmers spread over the soil after a harvest. Some shells become—guess what? Kitty litter. But most of them are burned as fuel for the mill.

Would you like to have a peanut mulch for your garden? To make it, crush the shells with a rolling pin.

Kitty litter can be made in the same way. To a cup of crushed shells, add one-half teaspoon of baking soda. It takes the bad smell out of cat waste.

Eat and Enjoy

Of course, peanuts are roasted too, and peanut butter is made from them. Both are good for you. Peanuts contain foods that give you energy—fat, starch, and sugar. They also contain the proteins that are needed to build muscle. Ounce for ounce they have as much food value as beef. And isn't it great that peanuts taste so good!

MAKE YOUR OWN PEANUT BUTTER
Ask a grown-up to help you make your own peanut butter. You can use raw or roasted peanuts without skins. Add one teaspoon of vegetable oil to one cup of peanuts. Then grind the mixture in a food processor or meat grinder.

POP!
Goes the Corn

Now for a science experiment that you can eat—an experiment with popcorn.

Although it's easy to pop corn, don't do any cooking unless a grown-up is helping you.

Put a tablespoon of vegetable oil in a pan. Add a tablespoon of popcorn and set the pan on a hot stove. When the kernels swell, shake the pan. Now watch them jump.

Some kernels explode—POP! They shoot right out of the pan.

Put a lid on the pan and keep on shaking it. Rat-a-tat, rat-a-tat-tat! The corn hits the lid. When all the corn has popped, yummy!

Though popcorn kernels seem dry, a lot of water is sealed up in them. When you heat the popcorn, the water inside it boils. As it turns to steam, it takes up more and more space. It expands. This makes the kernels swell and split. The steam shoots out, and POP! Air rushes in. It fills the space left by the steam. This makes the corn light and puffy.

Pop some more, but this time pop a teaspoon of kernels. Be sure to get a grown-up to help you.

Then pour the popped corn into a measuring cup. How much do you have now? Usually you get half a cup. That's 24 teaspoonsful—enough for a nice snack. But do you really have 24 times more popcorn? No, you still have the same number of kernels. After they pop, they just take up more space.

Puzzle of the Puff

Did you notice that raw popcorn sinks? But drop puffy popped corn into water and it floats. Why? Not because it's lighter—adding air doesn't make popcorn lighter. Air bubbles just make the kernels bigger. Puffed up kernels are less dense —that is, less compact—they are lighter than water. That's why they float. Being more compact, the raw kernels are heavier than water. So they sink.

Try this: Drop some raw kernels in a glass of soda water. Watch the bubbles gather on them. These bubbles make the kernels float—just as air bubbles do inside puffy popped corn. When the kernels reach the top of the water, their bubbles break, and they sink. After picking up more bubbles, up they come again.

Do Soaked Kernels Pop?

When a kernel is soaked, the skin gets loose and splits. If you try to pop it, nothing happens. The soaked kernel is like a pot of boiling water without a cover. The steam gets out easily, so there is no explosion—no pop.

Do Frozen Kernels Pop?

When popcorn is frozen, the water inside the kernels turns to ice. It doesn't leak out, and so the kernels pop. But see for yourself. Freeze some kernels in a plastic bag, then pop them—and eat them.

How Long Does Popcorn Keep?

Popcorn does not spoil if it is kept in a dry, cool place. Scientists have found that the kernels keep for years. They might even keep to the year 4000!

Scientists discovered some very old popcorn kernels in a place called Bat Cave, in New Mexico. Indians who lived in the cave long ago grew the popcorn. Tests showed that it was 2,000 years old. Yet after all that time, the popcorn was still good—it popped!

Corn Tales

The explorers of long ago who came to America from Europe had never seen corn. They were amazed at how much food could be produced by planting the kernels from just one ear. From their reports, we know the popcorn plant of the Indians was very much like the one we grow today. This plant has two ears, each with about 500 kernels. If all are used as seeds and all grow, there will be a thousand new plants, each with two ears—enough to feed a family for a long time.

Popcorn was not the only corn of the Indians. In some places native Americans grew sweet corn, the kind that we usually eat today. Indians also grew dent corn, which is now raised for farm animals.

Both kinds of corn grow taller than popcorn and both have more than two ears on each plant. Sweet and dent corn ears have more kernels on them than popcorn. Their kernels are bigger, too. But they do not pop.

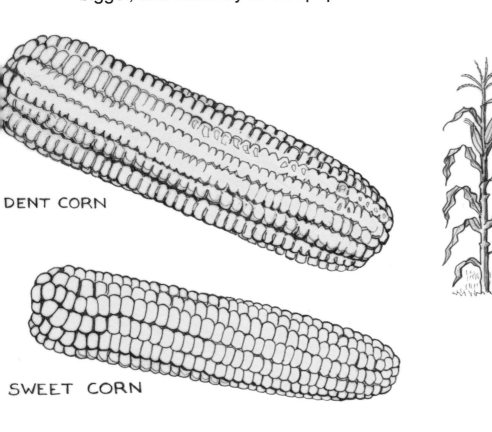

DENT CORN

SWEET CORN

POPCORN

Popcorn, Pilgrim Style

Did you know that popcorn was part of the first Thanksgiving feast? Indians brought it to the Pilgrims as a gift. The Pilgrims had never seen corn, but thanks to the Indians, they soon learned to eat it and grow it.

The Indians ate their popped corn plain, but the Pilgrims put cream and sugar on it. They liked it so much that way they ate it nearly every morning for breakfast.

Now we have many kinds of puffed cereals, but the first one was popped corn. Why not try some, Pilgrim style?

Let's Have a Party!

People everywhere give parties after the harvest. But there's no need to wait until then, for any time is a good time for a party with peanuts and popcorn. Where will you have the party? At home? At school? Wherever you have it, you will need grown-up help in planning, buying the food, and running the party.

Here's a game to start the fun.

Guess How Many

Show your friends a small jar filled with a cup of popcorn kernels. Then ask them to guess how many kernels are in it. Tell them you know the number and you will give the popcorn as a prize to the one who makes the best guess.

Do you count all the kernels in the jar? That would take a long time. Before the party, you can count the number in 1 teaspoonful. Say it holds 40 kernels. Next you pour 1 cup of popcorn into the jar. Well, 1 cup holds 48 teaspoons, and $48 \times 40 = 1920$.

Does anyone guess a number that big?

44

Will you pop corn at the party? Or roast peanuts? Here are some treats you can get ready before your friends come.

Rainbow Popcorn

Any flavoring such as
   vanilla, maple, anise

1 cup popped corn
Food coloring
2 cups water

Add a few drops of food coloring—any one you like—to the water. Make the color dark. Then add 1/2 teaspoon of vanilla or maple flavoring, or a few drops of anise oil. (Anise oil gives a licorice taste.) Soak the popped corn in the colored water for a few hours until it is colored. Then dry it on paper towels and pack it into a plastic bag.

Repeat the recipe using different colors and flavors. Your friends will have fun tasting them all.

Peanut Butter Chewies

1/2 cup crunchy peanut
   butter

3 tablespoons honey

1 teaspoon vanilla

3/4 cup instant nonfat dry milk

pinch of salt

3 tablespoons confectioners sugar

1/2 cup finely chopped unsalted
   roasted peanuts

Mix everything but the nuts in a bowl. Wet your hands and shape 1-inch balls from the mixture. Roll them in the chopped peanuts and the candy is ready.

You can serve a mix of peanuts, popcorn, and raisins, too. Apples go great with this mixture. So do apple slices spread with peanut butter.

Tongue Twisters

While munching and crunching on the treats, your friends can try these tongue twisters:

How many shreds can you get from sixty shells if you shred the unshred shells with a shredder?

How many pecks of popcorn does a popcorn popper pop when it pops a pound of popcorn kernels?

Put the Peanuts on the Plant

If you want an action game, here's one that's like pinning the tail on the donkey. Instead of a picture of a donkey and tails, you use a picture of a peanut vine with its underground parts.

Before the party, draw the picture on a big sheet of paper. Use tape to stick it on the wall. Get one peanut ready for each player. Take a paper clip and unbend it so it is L-shaped. Stick the bottom through a peanut shell. Put some sticky tape on the top of the clip, leaving about an inch of tape free. Now the peanut can be stuck on the vine.

46

When the game starts, the players line up, each with a peanut. One after another they are blindfolded, turned around, and given a chance to try to stick the peanut in the right place. Whoever gets it in the right place gets extra peanuts as a prize.

47

Riddle-Go-Round

And here are some special peanut and popcorn riddles.

1. What is the best thing to put into a ball of popcorn?

2. If it took a farmer two days to dig up the peanuts in two fields, how long would it take four people to dig up the same two fields?

3. How can you turn peanuts into pigs?

4. There's something that's made from peanuts and it's put in a jar.
   But how do you spell it
   Without using an *r?*

5. Why are peanut plants like men with mended pants?

6. How can you get popcorn to pop without heating it?

7. How can you divide 139 peanuts equally among 5 people?

8. How can you put 139 kernels of popcorn into 2 bags, each with more than 70 grains in it?

   No one will get all the answers, but everyone will have fun. You will have a great party.
